50 Best
Mashed
Potatoes

Sarah Reynolds

A John Boswell Associates/King Hill Productions Book
Broadway Books/New York

BROADWAY

50 Best Mashed Potatoes. Copyright © 1997 John Boswell
Management, Inc., and King Hill Productions. All rights reserved.
Printed in the United States of America. No part of this book may
be reproduced or transmitted in any form or by any means, elec-
tronic or mechanical, including photocopying, recording, or by any
information storage and retrieval system, without written permission
from the publisher. For information, address Broadway Books, a
division of Bantam Doubleday Dell Publishing Group, Inc.,
1540 Broadway, New York, NY 10036.

Broadway Books titles may be purchased for business or
promotional use or for special sales. For information, please write
to: Special Markets Department, Bantam Doubleday Dell
Publishing Group, Inc., 1540 Broadway, New York, NY 10036.

Broadway Books and its logo, a letter B bisected on the
diagonal, are trademarks of Broadway Books, a division of
Bantam Doubleday Dell Publishing Group, Inc.

Library of Congress Cataloging-in-Publication Data

First Edition

Illustration & design by Richard Oriolo

ISBN 0-7679-0043-X

99 00 01 10 9 8 7 6 5 4

Contents

Introduction

Mashed potatoes have to be the ultimate comfort food. For a while, when restaurant food was very precious and pretentious, mashed potatoes were rarely seen in public, though they were always scooped up greedily in the privacy of the home. As upscale diners became popular, highlighting what people really like to eat and bringing back the basics—that is, meat loaf or roast chicken and mashed potatoes—the smooth spuds moved out of the kitchen and onto the dining table. And that was only the beginning. Savvy chefs, not a group to ignore a good thing, took what was great and made it even better, going beyond the ordinary whipping in of butter and milk or cream to experiment with herbed olive oils, roasted garlic, chipotle chiles, and all sorts of other tasty additions.

Mashed potatoes, the most popular side dish in many fine restaurants, are currently enjoying tremendous favor. I don't know anyone of any age who doesn't like them. Gone are the days when whipped spuds were considered to be out of date, too fattening, or boring. We might be willing to skip dessert, but bring on a bowl of creamy whipped potatoes and let us dig in. Actually, when you think about it, mashed potatoes are held in such high esteem that a song and a dance are named after them!

As with any dish, even something as simple as mashed potatoes can be merely good or elevated to great. Following, besides fifty of the best mashed potato recipes you've ever seen, is some information about the ingredients and techniques, which will guarantee you smashing—or is it mashing?—success.

Types of Potatoes

Since mashed potatoes are essentially simple, the flavor and texture are largely dependent upon which potato you choose. In the United States, potatoes are generally divided into four basic categories: russets, long whites, round whites, and reds. A potato's function is largely determined by its starch content. The amount of starch determines whether a potato will be floury and mealy or waxy. Floury potatoes, like russets, are high in starch and low in water, which makes them the best for mashing. Starch is granular, so they naturally fall apart when boiled, making it easy to avoid lumps, and their low moisture content helps them to absorb all the good things (such as butter, milk, and cream) you add after they are cooked.

All-purpose potatoes have a medium starch content, which makes them good for mashing and for many other uses as well. Waxy potatoes, such as red-skinned varieties, are low in starch and high in water content. When cooked, they hold their shape and remain firm, so they are prime candidates for boiling and roasting, but they are used for mashing, too. Many varieties have very good flavor.

Potatoes come in almost infinite variety. Some are basic and have been around for a long time. Other heirloom and imported potatoes are becoming more common, offering us more alternatives of texture and flavor.

Russets: A.k.a. baking potatoes. Idahos are a particularly high grade of russet potato, though in fact they are grown in Maine and Oregon as well as in the state of Idaho. Russets have a rough brown skin, are oblong in shape, and are starchy, or floury. High in starch and low in moisture, they fall apart when cooked, which makes them ideal for mashing. Their dry, mealy texture makes very light, fluffy mashed potatoes. They are also excellent for baking and for French fries. The Russet Burbank, named for its developer Luther Burbank, the famous horticulturist, is the most common variety.

Long Whites: Oblong, with a light tan, thin skin, these are considered to be an all-purpose potato, which means they have a medium starch content. They are good for mashing, boiling, baking, and roasting. They were developed in

California and are grown in other western states. White Rose is a popular variety.

Round Whites: Grown in the Northeast, these are the light-skinned, ivory-fleshed round potatoes we think of as all-purpose. With a medium starch content, they can be used for most any purpose but do make a good mashing potato. Katahdin, Kennebec, Superior, and Irish Cobbler are well-known varieties.

Round Reds: These round, red-skinned potatoes, which have become a popular mashing potato, are frequently called boiling potatoes, with peeling not necessary. Waxy and smooth-skinned, they have a low starch content. When treated with care and not overworked, they make very flavorful mashed potatoes. Some variety names are Red Pontiac, Red La Soda, La Rouge, and McClure. Small red potatoes are often incorrectly called "new potatoes," a term that refers to any variety of potato that is freshly dug and not stored.

Yellow-flesh Potatoes: With their deep yellow color and firm but creamy texture, these all-purpose potatoes are a favorite with many chefs. They have a buttery taste, making them taste rich with less added fat. Yukon Golds have become the most well known and widely recognized type. Other varieties, such as Yellow Finns, La Reine, and Dutch Yellow, are not widely available yet, though they appear from time to time.

Purple Potatoes: At first glance, the color of these potatoes is truly startling and somewhat bizarre. Dark, almost black outside, they really are a deep purplish blue inside. Now becoming more common even in supermarkets, they can certainly add something extra to the color on a plate of food and are fun to serve, especially to friends who are unfamiliar with them. Peruvian Blue potatoes are the most flavorful variety. These medium-starch potatoes are considered to be all-purpose and good for mashing.

Other Varieties: Fingerling potatoes, named for their small, slim, fingerlike shape, tend to have very fine flavor. Fingerlings can be used for mashed potatoes. A few varieties are Ruby Crescent, Ozette Indian, and Lady Fingers. Look for these at farmers' markets, as they are cultivated by small independent and organic growers.

Sweet Potatoes

If you've ever been confused about the difference between sweet potatoes and yams, here's the true story.

Sweet Potatoes: Sweet potatoes are commercially grown in this country, and they are what you normally see in the supermarket. They come in two varieties: One has dark skin and sweet, deep orange flesh that is moist when cooked. It's what we mistakenly call a yam; in fact, to further confuse matters, some varieties are labeled yams. The other variety, which is less commonly seen, has a light skin and beige to ivory flesh that is not as sweet. When cooked, it is drier and more crumbly. Canned and frozen sweet potatoes are frequently labeled yams, whatever their actual provenance.

When sweet potatoes are featured in recipes in this book, the darker-skinned, deep orange variety should be used.

Yams: These are actually a different plant species, related to the cassava, and are seldom grown in the United States. They range from the size of a small potato up to seven feet! The color ranges from off-white to brown. They can sometimes be found in specialty food shops or ethnic food markets.

How to Buy and Store Potatoes

Select potatoes that are firm and smooth. Potatoes uniform in size will cook more evenly. To prevent waste when peeling, choose potatoes with fairly regular shapes. Avoid any that have wrinkled or wilted skins, soft dark areas, cut surfaces, or a green cast.

Store potatoes in a dry, dark, cool place, but not in the refrigerator. If potatoes are refrigerated, their starch turns to sugar, which makes them sweet and mushy. A temperature between 45°F. and 50°F. is ideal. When exposed to strong light—either sunlight or overhead light—potatoes develop a greenish tinge, which makes them bitter. If a potato is green, be sure to pare the colored part away. (Green potatoes are safe to eat as long as this part is removed.) If the green portion is extensive, then it's best to throw the potato away. Store potatoes with whatever dirt is clinging to them; it will help them last longer.

How to Cook and Mash Potatoes

Peel potatoes with a swivel-bladed vegetable peeler. If you prefer to leave the skin on, scrub the potatoes well with a vegetable brush under cold running water. The peel adds fiber and nutrients as well as interesting texture and sometimes color, but there is some controversy over whether the peel retains pesticides. With organic potatoes, you need not worry.

Before cooking, cut the potatoes into quarters or large chunks. If you aren't cooking them immediately, hold them in a bowl of cold water to prevent them from turning brown.

Place the potatoes in a large saucepan and add enough cold water to cover them by 1 inch. Bring to a boil, cover, and cook until the potatoes are tender; a knife or fork inserted in the center of a potato piece should slip out easily. Do not overcook potatoes to the point where they start to fall apart, or they will make gluey, waterlogged mashed potatoes. Most of the recipes in this book suggest 15 to 20 minutes, but exact cooking time will vary depending on the size of the potato chunks and what time of year it is (that is, how long after harvesting), so check them occasionally to avoid overcooking.

As soon as they are tender, drain the potatoes in a colander and return them while hot to the saucepan. (When they are whipped with an electric mixer, you'll find it easier to transfer them to a bowl.) Some recipes call for drying the cooked potatoes over low heat so they will absorb more butter or liquid, but as long as they are well drained, this step can usually be eliminated. Mash the potatoes and then gradually add the liquid, mashing the potatoes until smooth and fluffy. I say "gradually," because too much liquid will make the potatoes soupy or gluey. The amount of liquid needed will vary, depending upon the kind of potato used, its starch content, and its freshness, so I've sometimes given a range of liquid. It's always a good idea to reserve some of the cooking water before draining the potatoes; it can be used if you need a little more moisture but don't want any additional fat.

The Mechanics of Mashing

What utensil should be used to mash potatoes? Everyone has a favorite way to mash, and there is no one absolutely right way to do it. My low-tech method is to mash potatoes the old-fashioned way—with a manual potato masher. Sometimes, for extra-light, fluffy whipped potatoes, I'll break them up with the masher and then beat in the liquid with an electric mixer.

Many chefs and food professionals prefer to use a ricer. This utensil, which looks like a giant garlic press, does make very light, lump-free mashed potatoes, and if you have one, by all means use it. It's my instrument of choice for the firmer Yukon Gold and red-skinned potatoes, which can become gluey if over-worked with a masher or an electric mixer.

One absolute rule that must be observed when mashing potatoes is: *Almost never use a food processor.* A processor is so powerful that it breaks down the starch molecules and turns cooked potatoes into wallpaper paste. Exceptions are sweet potatoes and white potato purees that have a high ratio of other vegetables or fruits added to them.

What to Add to Mashed Potatoes

The liquid used for mashing potatoes generally should be hot. There are some cases where this rule doesn't apply, as when using buttermilk, which will curdle if heated. Milk is the most common liquid added to mashed potatoes. The potato cooking water, low-fat milk, skim milk, buttermilk, and yogurt can be used for flavorful, lower-fat alternatives. Half-and-half and heavy cream are luxurious additions that produce what I consider to be rich, special-occasion mashed potatoes.

For richness and flavor, butter is a favorite addition, and olive oil has become very popular. Modest quantities of extra-virgin and flavored olive oils will add lots of flavor. Cream cheese and sour cream provide richness as well as flavor. Add-in possibilities are endless, limited only by your imagination. All kinds of cheeses, sautéed or roasted vegetables, herbs, cooked bacon or ham, hot peppers, grated citrus zests, toasted seeds, toasted coarse bread crumbs, flavored oils, and spices are just some of the many additions that can be stirred into mashed potatoes.

Reheating Mashed Potatoes

Mashed potatoes are like pasta; they should be eaten immediately. Since that's not always possible, they can be reheated by stirring them over very low heat, or they can be held and kept hot in a double boiler. Many people achieve very successful results reheating the potatoes in a covered glass or ceramic bowl or casserole in a microwave oven. Of course, fresh is best. For convenience, I have included an entire chapter of "Make- Ahead Mashed Potatoes."

A Few Facts about Potatoes:

- One medium potato contains about 110 calories and virtually no fat, is high in vitamin C and minerals, and is a great source of complex carbohydrates and fiber.
- One pound of potatoes will yield about 2 cups mashed potatoes to serve 2 to 3 people.
- Use 2 medium baking potatoes or 3 medium all-purpose potatoes for approximately 1 pound of potatoes.
- Leftover mashed potatoes make a great soup thickener.
- Save potato cooking water as a base for soups, especially vegetarian soups.
- Potato cooking water is excellent for homemade breads. Yeast thrives on mashed potatoes or potato water, one reason that potato rolls and doughnuts are so light.

Whether you make mashed potatoes or do the "Mashed Potato," or even if you just eat them, as long as you love them, read on.

Mashed Potatoes
Better than Mom's

Here are eight traditional mashed potato recipes, ones that any mother would be proud to serve. The Best Ever Mashed Potatoes are the all-time classic version. Rich and Creamy Mashed Potatoes are luxurious, enriched with somewhat modest amounts of butter and cream. For calorie watchers, Lean and Luscious Mashed Potatoes and Buttermilk Mashed Potatoes taste good enough to satisfy anyone's craving for creamy mashed potatoes while leaving out excess fat and calories. Sour Cream and Chive Mashed Potatoes combine the classic baked potato toppings with mashed potatoes—a match made in heaven!

The Best Ever Mashed Potatoes

This is the basic version of mashed potatoes that we all know and love. It goes with virtually any meat, poultry, or fish, not to speak of your favorite beef, chicken, or lamb stew.

2 pounds baking potatoes, peeled and quartered
½ to ¾ cup hot milk
3 tablespoons butter, cut up
¾ teaspoon salt
¼ teaspoon freshly ground pepper

1. Place the potatoes in a large saucepan and add enough cold water to cover by 1 inch. Bring to a boil, reduce the heat, cover, and cook 15 to 20 minutes, or until tender. Drain the potatoes in a colander.

2. Return the hot potatoes to the pan and mash until smooth with a potato masher. Gradually add ½ cup milk, the butter, salt, and pepper, mashing the potatoes until fluffy, adding the remaining milk if necessary.

Rich and Creamy Mashed Potatoes

Serves 4 to 6

These are indulgent and worth the splurge. Because they are so special, I prefer to serve them with leaner meats and roast chicken or turkey.

2 pounds baking potatoes, peeled and quartered
½ cup heavy cream
¼ cup milk
5 tablespoons butter, cut into small pieces
¾ teaspoon salt
¼ teaspoon freshly ground pepper

1. Place the potatoes in a large saucepan and add enough cold water to cover by 1 inch. Bring to a boil, reduce the heat, cover, and cook 15 to 20 minutes, or until tender. In a small saucepan, heat the cream and milk over low heat until hot.

2. Drain the potatoes. Return to the pan and mash with a potato masher until smooth. Add the butter, salt, and pepper. Gradually add the hot milk mixture, mashing the potatoes until fluffy.

Lean and Luscious Mashed Potatoes

Because these mashed potatoes, whipped with the potato cooking water rather than milk, cream, or loads of butter, are so light, they take well to dishes that have a lot of sauce or gravy. A small pat of butter on top adds just a touch of richness.

2 pounds baking potatoes, peeled and quartered

2 large shallots, thinly sliced

1 teaspoon salt

½ cup plain nonfat yogurt

⅛ teaspoon freshly ground pepper

Dash of freshly grated nutmeg (optional)

1½ tablespoons butter, cut into 4 slices

1. Place the potatoes and sliced shallots in a large saucepan and add enough cold water to cover by 1 inch. Add ½ teaspoon of the salt. Bring to a boil, reduce the heat, cover, and cook 15 to 20 minutes, or until tender. Reserve ¾ cup of the cooking water. Drain the potatoes and shallots.

2. Return the hot potatoes and shallots to the pan. Mash until smooth with a potato masher. With an electric mixer on medium speed, beat in the yogurt and enough reserved cooking water to make the potatoes fluffy. Beat in the remaining salt, the pepper, and the nutmeg. If necessary, stir the potatoes over low heat until hot. Serve the potatoes with a pat of the butter on top of each serving.

Buttermilk Mashed Potatoes

Serves 4

Buttermilk contains only 1 or 1½ percent butterfat. It has a rich, nutty taste that makes these mashed potatoes taste so rich you won't miss the fat.

   2 pounds baking potatoes, peeled and quartered
   1½ teaspoons salt
   1 to 1¼ cups buttermilk
   ¼ teaspoon freshly ground pepper
   2 tablespoons chopped parsley

1. Place the potatoes in a large saucepan and add enough cold water to cover by 1 inch. Add 1 teaspoon salt. Bring to a boil, reduce the heat, cover, and cook 15 to 20 minutes, or until tender. Drain the potatoes in a colander.

2. Place the potatoes in a bowl and mash with a potato masher until fairly smooth. Gradually add 1 cup buttermilk, beating the potatoes with an electric mixer on medium speed until smooth and fluffy, adding more buttermilk if necessary. Stir in the remaining salt, the pepper, and parsley.

Buttery Smashed Spuds

Serves 4

Yukon Gold potatoes, noted for their yellow color and excellent flavor, are now more frequently available in most markets. In this recipe, the skins are left on the potatoes for extra texture. These are perfect with meat loaf and hamburgers.

2 pounds Yukon Gold potatoes, quartered

6 tablespoons butter, cut into small pieces, at room temperature

¾ teaspoon salt

¼ teaspoon freshly ground pepper

1. Place the potatoes in a large saucepan and add enough cold water to cover by 1 inch. Bring to a boil, reduce the heat, cover, and cook 15 to 20 minutes, or until tender. Reserve ⅔ cup cooking water. Drain the potatoes.

2. Return the hot potatoes to the pan. Mash with a potato masher until fairly smooth. Add the butter, salt, and pepper, mashing until the butter melts. Gradually add enough of the reserved cooking water to moisten to the desired consistency, mashing the potatoes until creamy.

Sour Cream and Chive Mashed Potatoes

Serves 4 to 6

If you like baked potatoes slathered with sour cream and chives, you'll love them with the same classic baked potato toppings mashed right in. These are especially good with steaks and roast beef.

2 pounds baking potatoes, peeled and quartered

¾ cup sour cream

3 tablespoons butter, cut into small pieces

¾ teaspoon salt

¼ teaspoon freshly ground pepper

¼ cup snipped chives

1. Place the potatoes in a large saucepan and add enough cold water to cover by 1 inch. Bring to a boil, reduce the heat, cover, and cook 15 to 20 minutes, or until tender. Reserve ¼ cup of the cooking water. Drain the potatoes.

2. Return the hot potatoes to the pan. Mash with a potato masher until smooth. Add the sour cream, butter, salt, and pepper. Mash until fluffy, adding some of the cooking water if necessary. Stir in the chives.

Mashed Potatoes with Browned Onions

Serves 4

*P*otatoes and onions are perfect partners. If you know time will be short before dinner, cook the onions a day ahead. Serve with roast chicken or pork.

3 tablespoons butter

1 pound Spanish onions, halved and thinly sliced

2 teaspoons cider vinegar

1½ pounds baking potatoes, peeled and quartered

½ cup hot milk

¾ teaspoon salt

¼ teaspoon freshly ground pepper

1. In a large skillet, melt the butter over medium-low heat. Add the onions, stirring to coat with the butter. Cover and cook 10 minutes, or until the onions soften and exude liquid. Uncover, increase the heat to medium, and cook 15 to 20 minutes longer, stirring frequently, until the onions are very soft, browned, and reduced to ¾ cup. Stir in the vinegar and set aside.

2. Place the potatoes in a large saucepan and add enough cold water to cover by 1 inch. Bring to a boil, reduce the heat, cover, and cook 15 to 20 minutes, or until tender. Reserve ¼ cup cooking water. Drain the potatoes.

3. Return the hot potatoes to the pan. Mash with a potato masher until smooth. Gradually add the hot milk, mashing the potatoes until smooth and fluffy, adding some of the reserved cooking water if necessary. Stir in the salt, pepper, and browned onions.

Colcannon

Colcannon is an Irish combination of potatoes, kale, and onions. Green cabbage is also commonly used in place of kale. If you substitute cabbage, try savoy cabbage, which has a sweet, mellow flavor. Serve with corned beef or chicken.

1½ pounds baking potatoes, peeled and quartered
3 tablespoons butter
1 medium onion, finely chopped
½ pound kale, stemmed and shredded
¾ cup hot milk
¾ teaspoon salt
¼ teaspoon freshly ground pepper

1. Place the potatoes in a large saucepan and add enough cold water to cover by 1 inch. Bring to a boil, reduce the heat, cover, and cook 15 to 20 minutes, or until tender.

2. Meanwhile, in a large skillet, melt 2 tablespoons of the butter over medium-low heat. Add the onion and cook, stirring frequently, until browned, about 10 minutes. Scrape the onion onto a plate. Add the kale and ¾ cup water to the skillet. Bring to a boil, reduce the heat, cover, and cook 10 minutes, or until the kale is tender. Drain off and reserve the cooking water.

3. Drain the potatoes. Return to the pan. Mash with a potato masher until smooth. Gradually add the hot milk, mashing the potatoes until fluffy, adding the reserved cooking water if necessary. Stir in the remaining 1 tablespoon butter, the onions, kale, salt, and pepper until blended.

Say Cheese When You
Mash

Cheese and potatoes go together like cookies and milk. Where would potatoes au gratin be without the cheese? They'd be just ordinary scalloped potatoes! This chapter explores the possibilities of this creamy duo, in ways that range from down-home to sophisticated.

Three-Cheese Mashed Potatoes, loaded with Cheddar, Romano, and Monterey Jack, have enough interest of their own to complement any simple meat. Creamy Cream Cheese Mashed Potatoes are rich and slightly tangy with cream cheese and sour cream. Southwestern Spuds with Cheddar Cheese and Corn, packed with chili powder, corn, scallions, and Cheddar and Jack cheeses, are full of flavor. Mashed Potatoes with Bacon, Greens, and Gorgonzola Cheese makes a great winter dish, hearty enough on its own to have for lunch or dinner.

Three-Cheese Mashed Potatoes

Potatoes and cheese are a perfect match, and the combination turns up in many favorite potato dishes. Cheese adds extra piquancy to the mild potato, while its creamy, melting texture makes mashed potatoes even smoother and more sumptuous than they already are. These go particularly well with ham or meat loaf.

1½ pounds baking potatoes, peeled and quartered
¾ cup milk
3 tablespoons butter, cut up
1 cup shredded extra-sharp Cheddar cheese
½ cup shredded Monterey Jack cheese
3 tablespoons grated Romano cheese
½ teaspoon salt
¼ teaspoon freshly ground pepper
⅛ teaspoon cayenne

1. Place the potatoes in a large saucepan and add enough cold water to cover by 1 inch. Bring to a boil, reduce the heat, cover, and cook 15 to 20 minutes, or until tender. Drain into a colander.

2. Meanwhile, in a small saucepan, heat the milk and butter over low heat until the butter melts and the milk is hot.

3. Return the potatoes to the pan. Mash with a potato masher. Add the hot milk and butter half at a time, mashing until blended. Reserving 2 tablespoons each of the Cheddar and Monterey Jack cheese, add the remainder of those cheeses and all the Romano to the potatoes, along with the salt, pepper, and cayenne. Stir until the cheeses are mixed in but not completely melted. Turn the potatoes into a heatproof serving dish or casserole. Sprinkle the reserved Cheddar and Jack cheeses over the top.

4. Preheat the broiler. Broil the potatoes 4 to 5 inches from the heat 1 to 2 minutes, until the cheeses are melted and bubbly. Serve at once.

Note: If you wish to make this ahead, set aside at room temperature for up to 2 hours or refrigerate up to 6 hours. Let return to room temperature before proceeding. About half an hour before serving, preheat the oven to 375°F. Bake the potato casserole 20 to 25 minutes, until the potatoes are heated through and the cheeses on top are melted and bubbly

Creamy Cream Cheese Mashed Potatoes

Cream cheese makes for extra-creamy, silken mashed potatoes. Feel free to use the reduced-fat variety, labeled "Neufchatel," if you prefer.

2 pounds baking potatoes, peeled and quartered
1 (3-ounce) package cream cheese, cut into small pieces, at room
      temperature
½ cup hot milk
¼ cup sour cream
¾ teaspoon salt
¼ teaspoon freshly ground pepper

1. Place the potatoes in a large saucepan and add enough cold water to cover by 1 inch. Bring to a boil, reduce the heat, cover, and cook 15 to 20 minutes, or until tender. Reserve ¼ cup cooking water. Drain the potatoes.

2. Return the hot potatoes to the pan. Mash with a potato masher until smooth. Add the cream cheese and ¼ cup milk, mashing the potatoes until the cream cheese is blended in. Add the remaining milk, sour cream, salt, and pepper. Mash the potatoes until fluffy, adding some of the reserved cooking water if necessary.

3. If the potatoes have cooled off too much, reheat them over low heat or in a glass or ceramic bowl, covered, in a microwave oven.

Ricotta Whipped Mashed Potatoes

Ricotta cheese and olive oil add a subtle Italian twist to mashed potatoes. These are particularly good with roast leg of lamb or lamb chops.

2 pounds baking potatoes, peeled and quartered
½ cup whole-milk ricotta cheese
3 tablespoons olive oil
¾ teaspoon salt
⅛ teaspoon freshly ground pepper

1. Place the potatoes in a large saucepan and add enough cold water to cover by 1 inch. Bring to a boil, reduce the heat, cover, and cook 15 to 20 minutes, or until tender. Reserve ¾ cup of the cooking water. Drain the potatoes.

2. Transfer the hot potatoes to a mixing bowl and mash them with a potato masher until smooth. Add ½ cup of the reserved cooking water, the ricotta cheese, olive oil, salt, and pepper and beat with an electric mixer on medium speed until fluffy, adding additional cooking water if necessary.

Southwestern Spuds with
Cheddar Cheese and Corn

Serves 6

Mexican *flavors are everywhere these days, even in mashed potatoes. These chili-spiked spuds, studded with corn, make a fine accompaniment to grilled or barbecued chicken.*

1½ pounds baking potatoes, peeled and quartered
3 tablespoons butter
1½ cups corn kernels, fresh, frozen, or canned
1 teaspoon chili powder
⅓ cup thinly sliced scallions
½ to ¾ cup hot milk
½ teaspoon salt
¼ teaspoon freshly ground pepper
1 cup shredded sharp Cheddar cheese
2 ounces pepper Jack cheese, finely diced

1. Place the potatoes in a large saucepan and add enough cold water to cover by 1 inch. Bring to a boil over high heat. Reduce the heat to medium, cover, and cook 15 to 20 minutes, or until the potatoes are tender.

2. Meanwhile, in a large skillet, melt the butter over medium heat. Add the corn kernels and cook, stirring constantly, 2 minutes, or until the corn is tender. Stir in the chili powder and scallions. Cook 1 to 2 minutes, until the scallions soften. Remove from the heat and set aside.

3. Drain the cooked potatoes in a colander. Return the hot potatoes to the pan and mash with a potato masher until fairly smooth. Gradually add ½ cup hot milk, the salt, and pepper, mashing the potatoes until fluffy. Add the remaining milk if necessary.

4. Return the pan to low heat and stir constantly until the potatoes are hot. Stir in the Cheddar and Jack cheeses and the corn mixture and serve.

Mashed Potatoes with Bacon, Greens, and Gorgonzola Cheese

Serves 4

Here's a substantial main-dish version of mashed potatoes that is a takeoff on a favorite French salad. Frisée is a curly, pale green, slightly bitter lettuce. If you can't find it, substitute curly endive or chicory, but use only the tender, lighter green inside leaves.

2 slices of sourdough bread

3 tablespoons olive oil

1 pound Yukon Gold or all-purpose potatoes, peeled and cut into 1-inch
    chunks

1 tablespoon Dijon mustard

1 tablespoon red wine vinegar

½ teaspoon salt

½ teaspoon freshly ground pepper

½ pound thick-sliced bacon, cut crosswise into 1-inch pieces

1 small red onion, chopped

1 large bunch of frisée, torn into bite-sized pieces (6 cups)

½ cup crumbled gorgonzola or other blue cheese

1. Preheat the oven to 400°F. Brush the bread slices on one side with 1 teaspoon of the olive oil. Cut into ½-inch cubes. Spread out on a jelly roll pan and bake 6 to 8 minutes, or until golden and crisp.

2. Place the potatoes in a large saucepan and add enough cold water to cover by 1 inch. Bring to a boil, reduce the heat, cover, and cook 10 to 15 minutes, or until tender. Drain the potatoes. Return to the pot and mash coarsely.

3. Meanwhile, in a small bowl, combine the remaining olive oil, the mustard, vinegar, salt, and pepper. Whisk until well blended. Set the dressing aside.

4. In a large skillet, cook the bacon over medium heat until crisp, about 6 minutes. With a slotted spoon, remove the bacon and drain on paper towels. Pour off and discard the drippings from the skillet.

5. Add 1 teaspoon of the reserved dressing and the red onion to the skillet. Cook until the onion softens, 3 to 5 minutes. Add the cooked onion and half of the remaining dressing to the potatoes and stir until combined.

6. In a large bowl, toss the frisée with the remaining dressing until coated. Add the croutons, bacon, and gorgonzola and toss gently. Divide the salad among 4 plates. Spoon the potatoes into the center of each and serve.

Mediterranean Mashed Potatoes with Goat Cheese and Olives

Serves 4

*F*ragrant herbs, tangy goat cheese, and salty black olives make for mashed potatoes that are truly addictive. For easy preparation, look for pitted kalamata olives in the deli section of your supermarket. These potatoes go particularly well with roast lamb and chicken.

1½ pounds Yukon Gold or all-purpose potatoes, peeled and quartered

1 tablespoon fresh thyme leaves or 1 teaspoon dried

4 garlic cloves, peeled

¼ cup hot heavy cream

4 ounces mild white goat cheese, crumbled

⅓ cup pitted kalamata olives, coarsely chopped

2 tablespoons extra-virgin olive oil

½ teaspoon salt

¼ teaspoon freshly ground pepper

1. In a saucepan, cover the potatoes and thyme with water. Bring to a boil, reduce the heat, cover, and cook 10 minutes. Add the garlic and cook 5 to 10 minutes longer, until the potatoes are tender. Reserve ⅓ cup cooking water. Drain the potatoes and garlic into a colander.

2. Return the hot potatoes and garlic to the pan. Mash with a potato masher until smooth. Stir in the cream, goat cheese, olives, olive oil, salt, and pepper. If needed, mix in enough of the reserved cooking water to make the potatoes fluffy.

Parmesan Pepper Mashed Potatoes

Serves 4

Freshly grated imported Parmesan cheese will really make a difference in this dish. So will good-quality, freshly grated black pepper. Set your pepper mill to a grind that is not too fine.

2 pounds baking potatoes, peeled and quartered
½ cup hot milk
3 tablespoons butter, cut into small pieces
½ cup freshly grated Parmesan cheese
½ teaspoon salt
½ teaspoon freshly ground black pepper
Dash of cayenne

1. Place the potatoes in a large saucepan and add enough cold water to cover by 1 inch. Bring to a boil, reduce the heat, cover, and cook 15 to 20 minutes, or until tender. Reserve ½ cup cooking water. Drain the potatoes.

2. Return the hot potatoes to the pan. Mash with a potato masher until smooth. Add the milk, butter, Parmesan cheese, salt, pepper, and cayenne. Place the pan over low heat and mash the potatoes until fluffy, adding the reserved cooking water as needed.

Make-Ahead
Mashed Potatoes

When you're pressed for time or just want to get the meal out of the way in advance, this is the chapter to turn to. These recipes allow you to do the work ahead, eliminating the need for last-minute preparations. One recipe is even made from leftover mashed potatoes.

Savory Mashed Potato Casserole, made more substantial with eggs and two kinds of cheese, will feed a crowd. Baked Stuffed Mashed Potatoes are everyone's favorite. Mexican Potato Pie can dress up even the plainest dinner. The Big Baked Potato Cake is brown and crusty, simple but impressive, an ideal accompaniment to just about any meat, poultry, or fish.

Pommes Duchesse

Serves 6

Thanks to the eggs, these classic French potatoes puff up and turn golden when baked. They are a traditional garnish to roasts and chops. Since they can be prepared ahead of time and baked shortly before serving, they are convenient for entertaining. These are traditionally piped out in mounds or a bordering strip. If you don't have a piping bag or a star tip, simply shape these into mounds with a couple of spoons; use one to scoop up the potato mixture and the other to scrape it off the first spoon.

2 pounds baking potatoes, peeled and quartered

4 tablespoons butter, melted

¼ cup hot milk

2 whole eggs, lightly beaten

2 egg yolks

½ teaspoon salt

⅛ teaspoon white pepper

Pinch of grated nutmeg

1. Place the potatoes in a large saucepan and add enough cold water to cover by 1 inch. Bring to a boil, reduce the heat, cover, and cook 15 to 20 minutes, or until tender. Drain the potatoes.

2. Press the potatoes through a ricer or a coarse sieve into the saucepan. Stir in 2 tablespoons of the melted butter and the milk. Let cool at least 10 minutes. (The mashed potatoes can be prepared ahead of time to this point and refrigerated, covered. Let return to room temperature before proceeding.)

3. Preheat the oven to 425°F. Adjust the oven rack to the upper third. Beat the whole eggs, egg yolks, salt, white pepper, and nutmeg into the mashed potatoes until well blended.

4. Spoon the potato mixture into a piping bag fitted with a large star tip. Pipe the potatoes into 12 swirls on a greased baking sheet. (Or use 2 spoons to make mounds.) Brush the potatoes with the remaining melted butter.

5. Bake the potatoes 15 minutes, or until browned. Serve immediately.

Variation

Potato Puffs with Cheddar Cheese: Stir 1 cup shredded sharp Cheddar cheese into the mashed potatoes along with the butter and milk in Step 2.

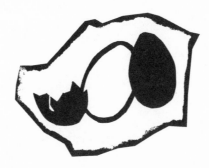

Baked Stuffed Mashed Potatoes

Everyone seems to love these classic stuffed potatoes. With a salad, they are filling enough to make a meal.

4 large baking potatoes (10 ounces each)
1 tablespoon butter
¼ cup chopped onion
1 fresh jalapeño pepper, seeded and minced
1 medium tomato, chopped
¼ cup hot milk
⅓ cup sour cream
⅓ cup finely diced sharp Cheddar cheese
¼ cup grated Parmesan cheese
½ teaspoon salt
⅛ teaspoon freshly ground pepper

1. Preheat the oven to 425°F. Prick the potatoes in 2 or 3 places with the tip of a small knife. Bake 1 hour, or until soft.

2. In a medium skillet, heat the butter over medium heat. Add the onion and jalapeño pepper. Cook, stirring occasionally, until softened, 3 to 5 minutes. Add the tomato and cook until the tomato has softened, about 2 minutes longer.

3. Holding the potatoes with a kitchen mitt or pot holder, cut a thin length-wise slice off the top of each. Scoop the potatoes into a bowl, leaving ¼-inch shells. Mash the pulp with a potato masher while it's still hot. Gradually add the milk, mashing until smooth. Stir in the sour cream, Cheddar cheese, 2 table-spoons of the Parmesan cheese, the salt, pepper, and cooked vegetables. Spoon the potato mixture back into the shells, mounding it to fill. Sprinkle ½ tablespoon

Parmesan cheese over the top of each stuffed potato. (If you wish, set aside for up to 2 hours at room temperature or refrigerate up to 24 hours. Let return to room temperature before proceeding.)

4. Place the potatoes in a small baking dish and bake 15 to 20 minutes, or until piping hot and lightly browned on top.

Savory Mashed Potato Casserole

Serves 8

This casserole is a good potluck dinner candidate. With the Boursin and Parmesan cheeses, it has distinctive taste and creamy texture. It can be made ahead and refrigerated overnight. Just be sure to let it come to room temperature before baking.

> 3 pounds baking potatoes, peeled and quartered
> 1 cup milk
> 1 package (5.2 ounces) soft garlic-herb cheese (Boursin), crumbled
> 2 eggs, lightly beaten
> ¾ cup grated Parmesan cheese
> ¼ cup chopped parsley
> ¾ teaspoon salt
> ¼ teaspoon freshly ground pepper

1. Place the potatoes in a large saucepan and add enough cold water to cover by 1 inch. Bring to a boil, reduce the heat, cover, and cook 15 to 20 minutes, or until tender. Drain the potatoes.

2. Return the potatoes to the pan and mash until smooth. Gradually add the milk, mashing the potatoes until fluffy. Let cool 10 minutes.

3. Stir the garlic-herb cheese, eggs, ½ cup of the Parmesan cheese, the parsley, salt, and pepper into the mashed potatoes, blending well. Turn into a greased deep 2-quart baking dish. Swirl the top with a spoon. Sprinkle with the remaining ¼ cup Parmesan cheese. (Cover and refrigerate if not baking immediately. Let return to room temperature before proceeding.)

4. About an hour before you plan to serve, preheat the oven to 375°F. Bake the casserole uncovered 45 to 50 minutes, or until hot throughout and browned on top.

Big Baked Potato Cake

Serves 6

This potato cake gets brown and crusty on the outside and remains soft and creamy inside. To dress it up, pass a bowl of sour cream and chives on the side.

>   2 pounds Yukon Gold or all-purpose potatoes, peeled and quartered
>   3 tablespoons olive oil
>   ½ teaspoon salt
>   ¼ teaspoon freshly ground pepper

1. Place the potatoes in a large saucepan and add enough cold water to cover by 1 inch. Bring to a boil, reduce the heat, cover, and cook 15 to 20 minutes, or until tender. Drain the potatoes.

2. Preheat the oven to 425°F. Return the potatoes to the pan and mash, leaving some chunks. Stir in 2 tablespoons of the olive oil, the salt, and the pepper.

3. In an 8- or 9-inch cast-iron skillet, heat the remaining 1 tablespoon oil over medium-high heat, swirling the oil to coat the sides of the pan. Add the potatoes and press with a spatula.

4. Transfer the skillet to the oven and bake the cake 40 to 45 minutes, or until well browned on the bottom. To serve, run a knife around the sides, place a serving plate over the skillet and using pot holders, carefully invert. Cut the cake into wedges and serve immediately.

Mashed Potato Cakes

Serves 4

What to do with leftover mashed potatoes? Try these savory cakes, which use mashed potatoes on the inside and freshly shredded potatoes on the outside for a crisp, brown exterior, creamy center, and double potato flavor. They make a perfect accompaniment to just about any food. For an extra-special brunch dish, serve them garnished with sour cream and thin strips of smoked salmon. Or see below how to combine them with more leftovers and turn them into a casual first course or light supper.

2 cups cold leftover mashed potatoes, or mashed potatoes made from
    1 pound of potatoes
2 scallions, finely chopped
2 tablespoons dry bread crumbs
1 egg white
⅛ teaspoon pepper
1 large Yukon Gold or all-purpose potato, scrubbed and shredded
2 tablespoons butter
1 tablespoon vegetable oil

1. In a medium bowl, combine the mashed potatoes, scallions, bread crumbs, egg white, and pepper. Stir until blended. Divide the potato mixture into 8 portions, about ¼ cup each.

2. Spread the shredded potato on a flat surface and place the potato cakes on the shreds, pressing and turning until coated with the shreds to make 8 round cakes about ¾ inch thick.

3. Heat 1 tablespoon butter and the oil in a large nonstick skillet over medium heat until hot. Add the potato cakes and cook until browned on the bottom, about 6 minutes. Add the remaining butter and turn the cakes over. Cook the cakes 6 minutes longer, or until browned. Remove the cakes to paper towels to drain. Serve immediately while hot and crisp.

Variations

Curried Vegetable and Potato Cakes: In a medium skillet, heat 1 table-spoon oil over medium-low heat. Add ½ cup shredded carrot, ½ cup finely chopped cauliflower, ½ cup thawed frozen peas, 2 teaspoons curry powder, and ¼ teaspoon salt. Cook, stirring often, until the vegetables are tender, about 6 minutes. Prepare the recipe for Mashed Potato Cakes, adding the vegetables to the mashed potatoes in Step 1. Divide into 8 portions, using about ⅓ cup for each. Follow directions for forming and cooking cakes in Steps 2 and 3 above. These are good served as a first course or side dish with a sauce made of ½ cup plain yogurt, 2 tablespoons chopped fresh mint, and ½ teaspoon grated fresh ginger.

Potato and Cod Cakes with Dill and Horseradish: In a medium bowl, combine 2 cups cold leftover mashed potatoes with 2 cups coarsely flaked cooked boneless cod fillet (or other firm, white fish), 1 egg, 2 tablespoons minced onion, 2 tablespoons chopped fresh dill, 1 tablespoon prepared white horseradish, ½ teaspoon salt, and ¼ teaspoon freshly ground pepper. Mix well. Shape into 8 cakes about 3 inches in diameter, using about ⅓ cup for each. Dredge the cakes in flour. Cook over medium heat in a large nonstick skillet in 1 tablespoon butter and 1 tablespoon oil, turning once, until browned and crusty, about 6 minutes per side.

Baked Potato and Broccoli Croquettes

Serves 8

While croquettes are traditionally fried, I find you can achieve excellent results and use less fat by baking them. These can be made ahead and refrigerated. Coat them with the crumbs just before baking. Two of these cakes, served with a salad, could make a vegetarian dinner.

1 pound all-purpose potatoes (3 medium or 2 large)
3 tablespoons butter
1 cup broccoli florets, finely chopped
½ cup shredded Gruyère or Swiss cheese
⅓ cup grated Romano cheese
2 tablespoons minced red onion
1 egg, lightly beaten
¼ teaspoon salt
⅛ teaspoon freshly ground pepper
½ cup dry bread crumbs

1. Place the whole potatoes in a large saucepan and add enough cold water to cover by 1 inch. Bring to a boil, reduce the heat, cover, and cook 30 to 35 minutes, or until tender. Drain the potatoes and let stand until cool enough to handle.

2. While the potatoes are cooling, melt 2 tablespoons of the butter over medium heat in the same saucepan. Add the broccoli and cook, stirring often, until bright green and crisp-tender, about 2 minutes.

3. Peel the cooked potatoes and place them in a large bowl. Mash with a potato masher, leaving the potatoes slightly chunky. Add the broccoli, Gruyère cheese, Romano cheese, red onion, egg, salt, and pepper. Stir until well blended.

(The recipe can be prepared in advance up to this point. Cover and refrigerate. Let return to room temperature and stir to lighten before proceeding.)

4. Preheat the oven to 400°F. Use the remaining 1 tablespoon butter to grease a large baking sheet. Divide the potato mixture into 8 equal portions. Shape each into a thick cake about 2 inches in diameter. Coat the cakes with bread crumbs and place on the baking sheet.

5. Bake the croquettes 25 to 30 minutes, turning once, until nicely browned and crispy on the outside.

Mexican Potato Pie

Serves 8

This savory "pie," cut into wedges, will dress up as humble a main dish as hamburgers. It's also substantial enough to serve four people on its own for dinner; just cut it in larger wedges and offer a tossed salad on the side. If you like spicy food, use pepper Jack cheese.

2 pounds all-purpose potatoes, peeled and quartered
2 tablespoons olive oil
4 scallions, chopped
2 eggs, lightly beaten
¾ cup shredded Monterey Jack cheese
1 can (4 ounces) chopped green chiles, rinsed and drained
1 teaspoon chili powder
½ teaspoon salt
⅛ teaspoon cayenne
3 tablespoons dry bread crumbs
2 tablespoons cornmeal
¾ cup shredded Cheddar cheese

1. Preheat the oven to 375°F. Place the potatoes in a large saucepan and add enough cold water to cover by 1 inch. Bring to a boil, reduce the heat, cover, and cook 15 to 20 minutes, or until tender. Drain the potatoes.

2. In the same saucepan, heat 1 tablespoon of the olive oil over medium-low heat. Add the scallions and cook until wilted, 1 to 2 minutes.

3. Return the potatoes to the pan with the scallions. Mash with a potato masher until smooth. Let the potatoes cool for 10 minutes. Stir in the eggs, Monterey Jack cheese, chiles, chili powder, salt, and cayenne.

4. Coat a 9-inch pie plate with ½ tablespoon of the remaining oil. In a small bowl, combine the bread crumbs and cornmeal. Sprinkle half over the pie plate to coat the bottom and sides. Spread half of the potatoes in the pie plate. Sprinkle with the Cheddar cheese and top with the remaining potatoes, spreading to cover the cheese. Sprinkle with the remaining crumbs and drizzle with the remaining ½ tablespoon oil.

5. Bake the pie for 45 minutes, or until browned. Let stand 5 minutes before cutting into wedges.

Mashed Potato Salad

This recipe has been adapted from Jim Fobel's book, Big Flavors (Clarkson Potter/Publishers). I include it here because it's such an unusual use of mashed potatoes, and it's so good. Perfectly seasoned, it will prove to be a great picnic potato salad that will disappear fast.

    3 pounds baking potatoes
    I tablespoon salt
    2 hard-boiled eggs, peeled
    ½ cup mayonnaise
    2 tablespoons spicy brown mustard
    I tablespoon cider vinegar
    I tablespoon sweet pickle juice
    ¾ teaspoon freshly ground pepper
    ½ teaspoon paprika
    ½ cup mixed sweet pickles, finely chopped
    3 scallions, minced
    ⅓ cup finely chopped parsley

1. Place the whole potatoes in a large pot and cover with water. Add 1 teaspoon of the salt. Bring to a boil. Reduce the heat and cook, partially covered, 35 to 45 minutes, or until tender, depending on the size. Drain the potatoes and let cool to room temperature.

2. In a small bowl, mash the eggs with a fork until finely chopped. Add the mayonnaise, mustard, vinegar, pickle juice, pepper, paprika, pickles, scallions, ¼ cup of the parsley, and the remaining 2 teaspoons salt. Stir until blended, cover, and refrigerate the dressing.

3. Peel the potatoes and cut into chunks. Place in a large bowl and mash coarsely with a potato masher, leaving the potatoes chunky. Add the dressing to the potatoes and stir until blended. Cover and refrigerate overnight.

4. To serve, place the potato salad in a serving bowl and garnish with the remaining parsley.

The Best-Dressed
Mashed Potatoes

Here are twelve contemporary recipes for "dressed up" mashed potatoes that contain some exciting pairings of flavors and stylish or slightly unexpected ingredients. They are anything but ordinary. Some of these recipes are homemade versions of what is served in the trendiest of restaurants. Others are just as special, but simple enough for weekday dinners. Any would make great dinner party side dishes. I've even included a couple of recipes for specialty items, such as basil-flavored oil; you can buy some of these in supermarkets, but they are cheaper to make at home.

Roasted Garlic Mashed Potatoes probably leap to the top of the list of everyone's all-time favorite mashed potatoes. Chunky Herb and Garlic Mashed Roasted Potatoes are simple to make and are coarsely mashed right in the roasting pan. Red, White, and Blue Mashed Potatoes with Bacon and Onion, basically a mashed potato salad, can be served at room temperature. Chantilly Mashed Potatoes are a rich, decadent version of mashed potatoes, flavored with Parmesan and Gruyère cheeses. Chipotle Mashed Potatoes with Cilantro Butter are slightly spicy and make a great side dish to go with something simple, like roast chicken. Potatoes Mashed with Garlic, Parsley, and Lemon make for an easy, delicious way to dress up plain mashed potatoes.

Mashed Potatoes with Mascarpone and Frizzled Leeks

Serves 4 to 6

Crisp leeks make a great topping for these creamy potatoes. Mascarpone, a rich, creamy sweet Italian cheese, is now produced in Wisconsin, and is widely available, even in supermarkets.

2 pounds baking potatoes, peeled and quartered

½ cup mascarpone or sour cream

1 tablespoon butter

½ teaspoon salt

¼ teaspoon freshly ground pepper

3 medium leeks (white part only), cut lengthwise into 1½ by ⅛-inch julienne
strips, rinsed, and dried

3 tablespoons flour

1 cup vegetable oil

1. Place the potatoes in a large saucepan and add enough cold water to cover by 1 inch. Bring to a boil, reduce the heat, cover, and cook 15 to 20 minutes, or until tender. Reserve ½ cup cooking water. Drain the potatoes.

2. Return the hot potatoes to the pan. Mash with a potato masher until smooth. Add the mascarpone, butter, ⅜ teaspoon salt, and the pepper. Mash until fluffy, adding cooking water as needed.

3. Toss the leeks in the flour until coated. In a medium skillet, heat the oil over medium heat until hot. Shake the excess flour off the leeks and fry them in the hot oil in 3 batches, stirring constantly to separate the strips, until they are crisp and very light golden, about 2 minutes per batch. Remove with a slotted spoon and drain on paper towels. Season the leeks with the remaining ⅛ teaspoon salt.

4. Stir the potatoes over low heat until hot. Turn into a serving dish. Scatter the frizzled leeks over the top and serve.

Roasted Tomato Mashed Potatoes

Roasted tomatoes are used in all kinds of dishes, like pasta and pizzas, so why not in mashed potatoes? To save time, roast the tomatoes a day or two ahead.

1½ pounds baking potatoes, peeled and quartered
½ cup hot milk
¼ cup finely slivered fresh basil
¼ teaspoon salt
⅛ teaspoon freshly ground pepper
½ recipe Oven-Roasted Tomatoes (recipe follows)
4 sun-dried tomato halves packed in oil, minced
2 tablespoons oil reserved after baking Oven-Roasted Tomatoes or from
        jar of sun-dried tomatoes

1. Place the potatoes in a large saucepan and add enough cold water to cover by 1 inch. Bring to a boil, reduce the heat, cover, and cook 15 to 20 minutes, or until tender. Drain the potatoes.

2. Return the hot potatoes to the saucepan and mash until smooth. Gradually add the hot milk, mashing the potatoes until fluffy. Stir in the basil, salt, and pepper. Stir the potatoes over low heat until hot.

3. Finely chop the roasted tomatoes. Remove the potatoes from the heat and stir in the roasted tomatoes, sun-dried tomatoes, and reserved oil. Season with additional salt and pepper to taste. Serve hot.

Oven-Roasted Tomatoes

Roasting tomatoes intensifies their flavor. These are fabulous as a garnish, part of an antipasto plate, or chopped and added to mashed potatoes, pasta, or sauces.

8 plum tomatoes
¼ cup extra-virgin olive oil
2 garlic cloves, crushed through a press
¼ teaspoon salt
¼ teaspoon freshly ground pepper

1. Preheat the oven to 350°F. Cut the tomatoes lengthwise in half. Place them cut sides up in a single layer in a shallow baking dish. In a small cup, combine the olive oil, garlic, salt, and pepper. Drizzle the garlic oil over the tomatoes.

2. Bake the tomatoes 1½ to 2 hours, or until very soft and shriveled, basting occasionally with any oil or juices in the pie plate. Let cool before using. Reserve any oil in the plate for cooking or flavoring.

Roasted Garlic Mashed Potatoes

Serves 4 to 6

These trendy mashed potatoes go wonderfully well with roast beef or a grilled steak. If you're a die-hard garlic fan, drizzle the top with Garlic-Flavored Olive Oil (page 53).

2 pounds baking potatoes, peeled and quartered

1 head of Roasted Garlic (recipe follows)

1 cup half-and-half

2 tablespoons butter, cut up

½ teaspoon salt

¼ teaspoon freshly ground pepper

1. Place the potatoes in a large saucepan and add enough cold water to cover by 1 inch. Bring to a boil, reduce the heat, cover, and cook 15 to 20 minutes, or until tender. Drain the potatoes.

2. Separate the cloves of roasted garlic and squeeze them to pop the garlic out of the skins. Place the garlic pulp in a medium saucepan. Pour in the half-and-half and cook over medium heat until hot. Remove from the heat and mash until fairly smooth.

3. Return the potatoes to the large saucepan. Mash until smooth. Add half of the hot garlic mixture and the butter. Mash again to blend well. Add the remaining garlic mixture, the salt, and pepper. Mash until the potatoes are light and fluffy.

Roasted Garlic

I large head of garlic
½ teaspoon olive oil

1. Preheat the oven to 375°F. Remove the loose, papery outer skins from the head of garlic, but do not peel. Cut off the very top of the head to just expose the individual cloves. Set on a square of heavy-duty aluminum foil and drizzle the olive oil over the garlic. Wrap the garlic in the foil.

2. Bake 45 minutes to 1 hour, or until the garlic is soft and pale golden but not browned. Let cool.

Garlic-Flavored Olive Oil   Makes about I cup

This popular flavored oil is available in most grocery stores, but in case you can't find it, here is a homemade version.

I tablespoon chopped fresh garlic
I cup olive oil

1. in a small saucepan, combine the garlic and oil. Cook over low heat until the garlic sizzles, about 10 minutes. Let cool.

2. Pour the garlic oil into a clean jar; cover with a lid. Refrigerate at least 2 hours before using. Store the oil in the refrigerator up to 2 weeks.

Note: If the oil solidifies when cold, simply let stand at room temperature or run the covered jar under warm water.

Pesto Mashed Potatoes

To get really fancy, substitute sun-dried tomato pesto, which you can buy in a jar, for half of the basil pesto. Divide the mashed potatoes in half and stir one kind of pesto into each, which will make one pale green and one light red. Serve them side by side.

> 2 pounds baking potatoes, peeled and quartered
> ¾ cup hot milk
> 6 tablespoons basil pesto, homemade (recipe follows) or purchased
> 3 tablespoons freshly grated Parmesan cheese
> ½ teaspoon salt
> ⅛ teaspoon freshly ground pepper

1. Place the potatoes in a large saucepan and add enough cold water to cover by 1 inch. Bring to a boil, reduce the heat, cover, and cook 15 to 20 minutes, or until tender. Drain the potatoes.

2. Return the hot potatoes to the pan. Mash with a potato masher until smooth. Gradually add the milk, mashing the potatoes until fluffy. Stir in the pesto, Parmesan cheese, salt, and pepper.

Basil Pesto Makes about 1 cup

This classic Italian sauce is so versatile, it's well worth keeping around. Homemade is easy if you use a food processor.

1 large garlic clove, sliced
2 cups packed fresh basil leaves
3 tablespoons pine nuts (pignoli)
⅓ cup freshly grated Parmesan cheese
¼ teaspoon salt
½ cup extra-virgin olive oil

1. In a food processor, mince the garlic. Add the basil, pine nuts, Parmesan cheese, and salt. Process until the basil is chopped.

2. With the machine on, gradually pour in the oil through the feed tube until blended. If not used right away, scrape the pesto into a clean jar, add enough additional oil to cover the surface, cover tightly with a lid, and refrigerate for up to 2 weeks.

Chipotle Mashed Potatoes with Cilantro Butter

Serves 4

Chipotle chiles are smoked jalapeños that are sold dried or canned in adobo sauce. I call for the canned variety here because the sauce is tasty, but if you only have dried, here's what to do: Place the dried chipotle in a small heatproof bowl and cover with boiling water. Let stand 20 to 30 minutes, until soft. Remove the chile, cut off the stem, and remove the seeds. Also scrape off any light colored "ribs" that you see clinging to the inside. Mince the chile as finely as you can.

Chipotles pack a lot of heat, so use them sparingly. If the one you have is on the large side, add half at a time to the mashed potatoes. As they say, you can always add, but you can't take away.

2 pounds baking potatoes, peeled and quartered

6 garlic cloves, sliced

4 tablespoons butter

3 tablespoons minced cilantro

¾ cup hot milk

1 chipotle chile in adobo sauce, minced

½ teaspoon salt

1. In a large saucepan, cover the potatoes and garlic with water. Bring to a boil, reduce the heat, cover, and cook 15 to 20 minutes, or until tender. Drain the potatoes and garlic.

2. While the potatoes cook, in a small saucepan over low heat, melt 2 tablespoons of the butter. Stir in the cilantro and remove from the heat.

3. Return the hot potatoes and garlic to the pan. Mash with a potato masher. Gradually add the milk, mashing the potatoes until fluffy. Stir in the chile, the remaining 2 tablespoons butter, and the salt. Place the hot potatoes in a serving dish. Swirl with the back of a spoon to make indentations and pour the cilantro butter over the top.

Mashed Potatoes with Wild Mushrooms

Serves 6

Half the mushrooms here are the fresh white button type, which add bulk and good mushroom taste without undue expense; the other half are for heightened flavor. Use any combination that you can afford here. A few fresh morels would be a delicious extravagance. These potatoes make a fine side dish to dress up plain roast beef.

4 tablespoons butter

½ pound small white mushrooms, thinly sliced

¼ pound shiitake mushrooms, stems removed, caps sliced

¼ pound cremini (Italian brown) mushrooms, thinly sliced

1 large shallot, minced

2 garlic cloves, minced

¾ teaspoon salt

1½ pounds Yukon Gold potatoes, peeled and quartered

½ cup hot half-and-half

2 tablespoons snipped fresh chives

¼ teaspoon pepper

1. In a large skillet, melt 2 tablespoons of the butter over medium heat. Add all the sliced mushrooms, shallot, garlic, and ¼ teaspoon salt. Cook, stirring frequently, until the mushrooms are tender and dry, about 12 minutes. Remove from the heat.

2. Place the potatoes in a large saucepan and add enough cold water to cover by 1 inch. Bring to a boil, reduce the heat, cover, and cook 15 to 20 minutes, or until tender. Reserve ¼ cup of the cooking water. Drain the potatoes.

3. Press the hot potatoes through a ricer or a coarse sieve back into the saucepan. Gradually stir in the hot half-and-half and enough reserved cooking water to make the potatoes fluffy.

4. Return the skillet with the mushrooms to medium heat and reheat them, stirring often. Blend the remaining 2 tablespoons butter and ½ teaspoon salt, the chives, and the pepper into the mashed potatoes. Add the hot mushrooms and stir to combine. Serve at once.

Herbed Mashed Potatoes with Chive Vinaigrette

Serves 4 to 6

These flavored potatoes use Basil Oil (page 62) or other herb-flavored olive oil, now available in most good supermarkets. Occasionally only cream will do; it makes these potatoes especially luscious.

2 pounds Yukon Gold or all-purpose potatoes, peeled and quartered

¾ cup heavy cream

1 teaspoon minced fresh thyme or ½ teaspoon dried

½ teaspoon minced fresh rosemary or ¼ teaspoon dried

¼ cup basil oil, homemade (page 62) or purchased, or other
    herb-flavored olive oil

3 tablespoons chopped parsley

¾ teaspoon salt

¼ teaspoon freshly ground pepper

1 teaspoon tarragon vinegar

2 tablespoons snipped chives

1. Place the potatoes in a large saucepan and add enough cold water to cover by 1 inch. Bring to a boil, reduce the heat, cover, and cook 15 to 20 minutes, or until tender.

2. In a small saucepan, combine the cream, thyme, and rosemary. Bring to a simmer over medium heat. Add 2 tablespoons of the basil oil, cover the pan, and set aside.

3. Reserve ½ cup cooking water from the potatoes and drain. Return the potatoes to the pan. Mash the potatoes until smooth. Gradually stir in the cream mixture until combined. Add some of the reserved cooking water if necessary, stirring the potatoes until fluffy. Stir in the parsley, salt, and pepper.

4. In the small saucepan (no need to rinse), combine the remaining 2 tablespoons oil and the tarragon vinegar. Whisk over low heat until warm. Stir in the chives. Reheat the potatoes, if necessary, by stirring over low heat. Make a well in individual servings of the potatoes with the back of a spoon. Spoon on the vinaigrette.

Basil Oil Makes about 1¼ cups

Flavored oils are a great way to add a wallop of flavor with little effort. At the moment, these are a favorite ingredient with many chefs. Besides using it as a flavoring, they often drizzle a thin stream of it over or around the plate as a light garnish. Many supermarkets now carry flavored oils, but if you can't find one, here is an easy homemade version. It will keep in the refrigerator for up to 2 weeks.

> 2 cups packed fresh basil leaves
> 1½ cups olive oil

1. Bring a small pot of water to a boil. Add the basil, stir to immerse all the leaves, and immediately drain into a colander. Rinse under cold running water until cool. Dry the basil well between sheets of paper towels.

2. In a blender or food processor, combine the basil with ½ cup of the olive oil. Puree until smooth. Pour into a clean canning jar. Add the remaining 1 cup oil, cover with the lid, and shake until blended. Let stand at room temperature for 1 day.

3. Strain the oil through a fine sieve lined with cheesecloth into a clean jar. Cover with the lid and store in the refrigerator. Use as needed.

Chunky Herb and Garlic Mashed Roasted Potatoes

Serves 4

These savory, coarsely mashed potatoes go with just about anything and are so good they're addictive. Don't expect these to be as moist as regular mashed potatoes. Because they're roasted, they are drier, but they contain bits of wonderful crispy brown potato, combining two pleasures in one.

1 pound Yukon Gold potatoes, peeled and cut into 1-inch chunks
½ pound red-skinned potatoes, cut into 1-inch chunks
4 garlic cloves, thinly sliced
2 teaspoons chopped fresh rosemary or ¾ teaspoon dried
½ teaspoon salt
¼ teaspoon freshly ground pepper
2 tablespoons olive oil
1 teaspoon balsamic vinegar

1. Preheat the oven to 425°F. In a shallow roasting pan, toss the potatoes with the garlic, rosemary, salt, pepper, and 1 tablespoon of the oil until evenly coated.

2. Roast the potatoes 35 to 40 minutes, stirring occasionally, until tender and golden brown.

3. Mash the potatoes coarsely with a potato masher in the roasting pan. Stir in the remaining oil and the vinegar. Season with additional salt and pepper to taste and serve at once.

Smashed Red Potatoes with Extra-Virgin Olive Oil

Serves 6

Versions of these potatoes have become very popular in restaurants. These make a great weekday addition to the dinner table, as no peeling of the potatoes is required! Regular olive oil can be used instead, for a less pronounced flavor.

2 pounds red-skinned potatoes, cut into 1-inch chunks
3 garlic cloves, sliced (optional)
¼ cup extra-virgin olive oil
¾ teaspoon salt
¼ teaspoon freshly ground pepper

1. In a saucepan, cover the potatoes and garlic with water. Bring to a boil, reduce the heat, cover, and cook 15 to 20 minutes, or until tender. Reserve ½ cup cooking water. Drain the potatoes and garlic.

2. Return the potatoes and garlic to the pan. Over medium heat, shake the pan 1 minute or until the potatoes are dry. Remove the pan from the heat. Mash the potatoes coarsely with a potato masher. Add the olive oil, salt, and pepper. Gradually stir in enough cooking water to make the potatoes fluffy.

Chantilly Mashed Potatoes

Chantilly *suggests whipped cream, and these mashed potatoes are covered with cheese-filled whipped cream and baked, making this an exceptionally rich dish for a special occasion. The potatoes can be mashed and placed in the baking dish up to 2 hours ahead; prepare the cream mixture and bake just before serving.*

2 pounds baking potatoes, peeled and quartered
½ cup hot milk
¼ teaspoon salt
¾ cup heavy cream
½ cup shredded Gruyère cheese
⅓ cup freshly grated Parmesan cheese

1. Place the potatoes in a large saucepan and add enough cold water to cover by 1 inch. Bring to a boil, reduce the heat, cover, and cook 15 to 20 minutes, until tender. Drain the potatoes.

2. Return the hot potatoes to the pan and mash with a potato masher. Gradually add the milk to the potatoes, mashing until smooth. Stir in the salt. Spread the potatoes in a greased shallow 2-quart gratin or baking dish and cover to keep warm.

3. Preheat the oven to 450°F. In a medium bowl, beat the cream with an electric mixer on high speed until stiff. Fold in the Gruyère and 3 tablespoons of the Parmesan cheese. Spread the cream over the top of the potatoes. Sprinkle the remaining Parmesan cheese over the top.

4. Bake 12 to 15 minutes, until the potatoes are hot and the top is well browned. Serve at once.

Red, White, and Blue Mashed Potatoes
with Bacon and Onion

These *patriotic potatoes are flavored with bacon, browned onions, and a splash of vinegar. They are better if left on the dry side, making this more like a mashed German-style potato salad.*

1 pound all-purpose potatoes, peeled and quartered

½ pound red-skinned potatoes, quartered

½ pound blue potatoes, peeled and quartered

6 slices of bacon, cut crosswise into ½-inch pieces

1 large onion, finely chopped

3 tablespoons cider vinegar

2 teaspoons Dijon mustard

1 teaspoon sugar

1 teaspoon salt

½ teaspoon freshly ground pepper

⅓ cup chopped parsley

1. Place all the potatoes in a large saucepan and add enough cold water to cover by 1 inch. Bring to a boil, reduce the heat, cover, and cook 15 to 20 minutes, or until tender.

2. In a medium skillet, cook the bacon over medium heat until crisp, 4 to 5 minutes. Remove the bacon with a slotted spoon to a paper towel-lined plate. Pour off all but 3 tablespoons of bacon drippings from the skillet.

3. Add the onion to the drippings and cook over medium-low heat, stirring occasionally, until it is soft and browned, about 10 minutes. Stir in the vinegar, mustard, sugar, salt, and pepper. Remove from the heat.

4. Reserve ⅓ cup cooking water from the potatoes. Drain the potatoes and return to the pan. Mash with a potato masher, leaving the potatoes chunky. Add cooking water as needed to moisten the potatoes. Stir in the bacon, the onion mixture, and ¼ cup of the parsley. Serve the potatoes warm or at room temperature, with the remaining parsley sprinkled on top.

Potatoes Mashed with Garlic, Parsley, and Lemon

Serves 4

The combination of garlic, parsley, and lemon zest dresses up plain mashed potatoes. Try this with blue potatoes if available, but peel them.

2 pounds Yukon Gold or red-skinned potatoes, quartered

½ cup hot milk

¼ cup extra-virgin olive oil

6 garlic cloves, very thinly sliced

2 teaspoons grated lemon zest

½ cup chopped parsley

¾ teaspoon salt

¼ teaspoon freshly ground pepper

1. Place the potatoes in a large saucepan and add enough cold water to cover by 1 inch. Bring to a boil, reduce the heat, cover, and cook 15 to 20 minutes, or until tender. Reserve ¼ cup cooking water. Drain the potatoes.

2. Return the hot potatoes to the pan and mash with a potato masher. Add the milk and mash until fluffy, adding reserved cooking water as necessary.

3. In a small skillet, heat the oil over medium-low heat. Add the garlic and cook, stirring constantly, until it turns just golden but not brown, about 2 minutes. Remove the skillet from the heat and stir in the lemon zest. Pour the garlic mixture into the potatoes. Add the parsley, salt, and pepper and mash over low heat until hot.

Mashed Potatoes
and…

What better way to eat vegetables than to combine them with mashed potatoes? Some of these vegetable combinations are smooth and pureed, and others are chunky with pieces of vegetables.

All kinds of vegetables are combined with mashed potatoes here—carrots, rutabaga, arugula, broccoli, squash, leeks, fennel, and spinach are just a few.

Confetti Mashed Potatoes are very colorful, dotted with zucchini, carrots, peas, corn, peppers, and scallions. Leek and Fennel Mashed Potatoes make a delicious, flavorful puree. Mashed Browns are a takeoff on hash browns, only easier, and are seasoned with peppers, onions, and a touch of cayenne pepper.

Smashed Potatoes and Carrots

Serves 4

This is a great way to get the benefits of two vegetables at once. To add a peppery flavor and a touch of color, add ½ cup chopped watercress leaves to the potatoes before mashing. Serve with roast turkey, chicken, or meat loaf.

1 pound all-purpose potatoes, peeled and cut into 1-inch chunks
1 pound carrots, peeled and thinly sliced
¼ cup hot milk
2 tablespoons butter
½ teaspoon salt
⅛ teaspoon freshly ground pepper

1. Place the potatoes and carrots in a large saucepan and add enough water to cover by 1 inch. Bring to a boil, reduce the heat, cover, and cook 15 to 20 minutes, or until tender. Reserve ¼ cup of the cooking water. Drain the potatoes and carrots.

2. Return the hot potatoes and carrots to the pan. Mash with a potato masher. Add the hot milk, butter, salt, and pepper. Mash until blended, adding some of the reserved cooking water if needed.

Mashed Potatoes with Rutabaga and Apples

Serves 6

Rutabaga has a mellow flavor similar to turnip, but sweeter. It usually comes coated with wax, which acts as a preservative. Because the skin is so tough, you usually have to peel rutabagas with a knife. It's a good idea to rinse it after peeling, to remove any wax still clinging. Here it's combined with potatoes and apples. You can leave the peel on the apples for extra color and fiber. With its mild sweetness, this dish is particularly good with pork, goose, and duck.

1 medium rutabaga (2 pounds), peeled and cut into ½-inch cubes

1 pound baking potatoes, peeled and quartered

3 tablespoons butter

2 McIntosh apples, peeled, cored, and thickly sliced

2 teaspoons honey

¾ teaspoon salt

¼ teaspoon freshly ground pepper

1. Place the rutabaga and potatoes in a large saucepan and add enough water to cover by 1 inch. Bring to a boil, reduce the heat, cover, and cook 20 minutes, or until the vegetables are tender. Drain in a colander.

2. While the vegetables cook, melt the butter in a large skillet over medium heat. Add the apples and cook, stirring occasionally, until tender and lightly browned, about 6 minutes. Stir in the honey, salt, and pepper. Remove the skillet from the heat.

3. Add the hot rutabaga and potatoes to the skillet. Mash with a potato masher until fairly smooth, with small pieces of rutabaga and apple remaining.

Winter Root Vegetable Puree

Serves 6 to 8

*T*his savory puree makes a wonderful addition to the Thanksgiving table. Here is one instance where the potatoes can be pureed in a food processor because the ratio of other vegetables is so high. The browned vegetable garnish adds extra flavor and texture as well as visual interest. This puree can be made up to 2 days ahead and reheated.

1 large celery root (2 pounds)
2 parsnips (½ pound), peeled and thinly sliced
1 medium white turnip (6 ounces), peeled and diced
1 pound baking potatoes, peeled and cut into 1-inch cubes
4 garlic cloves, thinly sliced
4 tablespoons butter, cut into small pieces
¾ teaspoon salt
¼ teaspoon pepper

1. Peel the celery root with a paring knife and cut it into 1-inch cubes. Place it in a large saucepan. Cover with cold water to prevent discoloration. Measure out 1 cup of combined celery root, parsnips, turnip, and potatoes and set aside. Add the remaining vegetables and garlic to the saucepan and add water to cover by 1 inch. Bring to a boil, reduce the heat, cover, and cook 15 to 20 minutes, or until tender.

2. While the vegetables cook, cut the reserved 1 cup vegetables into ¼-inch dice. In a small skillet, melt 2 tablespoons of the butter over medium heat. Add the diced vegetables and cook, stirring often, until browned and tender, 10 to 12 minutes. Remove from the heat.

3. Reserve ¾ cup of the cooking water. Drain the vegetables well in a colander. Transfer the vegetables to a food processor. Add the remaining 2 tablespoons butter, the salt, and the pepper. Puree until smooth, scraping the bowl frequently and adding some of the reserved cooking water if necessary, until creamy.

4. Scrape the puree into a saucepan and stir over low heat until hot. Turn into a serving dish. Reheat the browned vegetables and spoon over the puree.

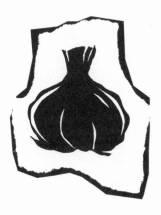

Mashed Potatoes with Broccoli and Hot Pepper Butter

Serves 4

Asiago is an Italian cheese with a rich, nutty flavor. Parmesan or Romano cheese can be substituted for it. Chicken broth is combined with water here to cook the potatoes, adding more flavor. (The leftover broth can be saved to make soup.) Include some of the tender broccoli stalk, sliced, as well as the florets. Serve with roast or broiled chicken.

1½ pounds baking potatoes, peeled and quartered

2 garlic cloves, sliced

1 can (13¾ ounces) chicken broth

3 tablespoons butter

2½ cups chopped broccoli (½ pound)

¼ teaspoon salt

¼ cup grated Asiago cheese

⅛ to ¼ teaspoon crushed hot red pepper flakes

1. In a saucepan, combine the potatoes, garlic, and chicken broth. Add water to cover by 1 inch. Bring to a boil, reduce the heat, cover, and cook 15 to 20 minutes, or until tender. Drain the potatoes and garlic, reserving ¾ cup of the cooking liquid.

2. In the same saucepan, melt 2 tablespoons of the butter over high heat. Add the broccoli and ¼ cup of the reserved broth. Bring to a boil, reduce the heat, cover, and cook until the broccoli is tender, about 4 minutes. Remove the pan from the heat and add the potatoes. Mash until smooth. Gradually add the reserved cooking broth, mashing the potatoes until fluffy. Add the salt and Asiago cheese and stir until blended.

3. In a small skillet, melt the remaining 1 tablespoon butter with the hot pepper flakes over medium heat. Turn the potatoes into a serving dish and drizzle the hot pepper butter over the top.

Mashed Potatoes and Arugula

Serves 4 to 6

Arugula *is a peppery dark salad green that adds a lovely zing to the blandness of mashed potatoes. Be sure to wash the arugula well, especially if it comes with the roots attached; they can be very sandy (trim off the roots before washing). Serve with chicken or steak.*

2 pounds baking potatoes

2 garlic cloves, sliced

3 tablespoons olive oil

2 bunches of arugula (about 5 ounces each), coarsely chopped

½ cup hot milk

¾ teaspoon salt

¼ teaspoon freshly ground pepper

1. Place the potatoes and garlic in a large saucepan and add enough water to cover by 1 inch. Bring to a boil, reduce the heat, cover, and cook 15 to 20 minutes, or until tender. Reserve ¼ cup of the cooking water. Drain the potatoes and garlic.

2. In the same saucepan, heat the oil over medium heat. Add the arugula and cook, stirring, until wilted. Continue to cook for 1 minute. Remove the saucepan from the heat, add the potatoes and garlic, and mash until smooth. Gradually add the milk, mashing the potatoes until fluffy, adding the reserved cooking water if needed. Season with the salt and pepper.

Confetti Mashed Potatoes

This simple, pretty combination is guaranteed to get the kids to eat their veggies. It's special enough for company, too. Substitute 2½ cups leftover chopped vegetables for a quick version. Serve with hot dogs, hamburgers, or meat loaf; it's good with roast beef, too.

2 pounds baking potatoes, peeled and quartered
3 tablespoons butter
½ cup finely diced zucchini
½ cup fresh or frozen corn kernels
½ cup frozen peas
½ cup shredded carrots
¼ cup finely diced red bell pepper
2 scallions, thinly sliced
¾ teaspoon salt
¾ cup hot milk
⅛ teaspoon freshly ground pepper

1. Place the potatoes in a large saucepan and add enough cold water to cover by 1 inch. Bring to a boil, reduce the heat, cover, and cook 15 to 20 minutes, or until tender.

2. While the potatoes cook, melt 2 tablespoons of the butter in a large skillet over medium heat. Add the zucchini, corn, peas, carrots, red bell pepper, and scallions. Cook, stirring frequently, until the vegetables are crisp-tender, about 4 minutes. Stir in ¼ teaspoon of the salt. Set aside.

3. Drain the potatoes and return them to the pan. Mash with a potato masher until smooth. Gradually add the hot milk, mashing the potatoes until fluffy. Stir in the remaining 1 tablespoon butter, and ½ teaspoon salt, the pepper, and the sautéed vegetables. Heat briefly and serve.

Mashed Potatoes with Butternut Squash

Serves 6

Roasting the squash is much easier than cooking it on top of the stove because you don't have to peel it first. The butter is browned for a nutty flavor. This goes particularly well with pork chops.

1 medium butternut squash (2 pounds), halved lengthwise and seeded

1 pound baking potatoes, peeled and quartered

3 tablespoons butter

¼ cup hot milk

½ teaspoon grated orange zest

½ teaspoon salt

Pinch of cayenne

1. Preheat the oven to 375°F. Line a jelly-roll pan with foil. Place the squash halves cut sides down on the foil. Bake 1 hour, or until tender. Turn the squash over and let cool.

2. Place the potatoes in a large saucepan and add enough cold water to cover by 1 inch. Bring to a boil, reduce the heat, cover, and cook 15 to 20 minutes, or until tender. Drain the potatoes.

3. In a small skillet, melt the butter over low heat. Cook until browned, about 2 minutes, and set aside.

4. Return the hot potatoes to the pan. Mash with a potato masher until smooth. Add the milk and mash until blended. With a spoon, scoop the squash into the potatoes. Add half of the browned butter, the orange zest, salt, and cayenne. Mash until blended. Reheat over low heat, stirring constantly, until hot. Turn into a serving dish and make indentations with the back of a spoon. Drizzle the remaining butter over the top.

Leek and Fennel Mashed Potatoes

Serves 6

If there are any feathery green tops on the fennel, reserve them to chop and sprinkle over these creamy, pale green mashed potatoes, which go well with fish, especially salmon.

2 medium leeks, white and light green parts only
1 large fennel bulb (1 pound), trimmed, cored, and thinly sliced
½ cup heavy cream
¼ cup milk
1½ pounds baking potatoes, peeled and quartered
3 tablespoons butter
¾ teaspoon salt
¼ teaspoon freshly ground pepper

1. Halve the leeks lengthwise and cut crosswise into ½-inch slices. Rinse well in a colander and let drain. In a medium saucepan, combine the leeks, fennel, cream, and milk. Bring to a boil, reduce the heat, and cook, partially covered, 15 minutes, or until the vegetables are soft. Drain off and reserve the liquid from the pan. In a food processor, puree the vegetables until smooth.

2. Place the potatoes in a large saucepan and add enough cold water to cover by 1 inch. Bring to a boil, reduce the heat, cover, and cook 15 to 20 minutes, or until tender.

3. Drain the potatoes. Return them to the pan and mash until smooth. Add the pureed vegetables, butter, salt, and pepper. Over low heat, mash until blended, adding enough reserved liquid to make the mixture fluffy. Turn into a serving dish and sprinkle with the chopped fennel tops.

Creamed Spinach Mashed Potatoes

Serves 6

One of my favorite childhood dinners was meat loaf, mashed potatoes, and spinach. I always mixed the potatoes and spinach together. Frozen creamed spinach makes for an especially easy version of this favorite combination.

1½ pounds baking potatoes
2 garlic cloves, thinly sliced
1 package (9 ounces) frozen creamed spinach, thawed
3 tablespoons butter
¼ cup grated Fontina or Parmesan cheese
¼ teaspoon salt
⅛ teaspoon freshly ground pepper

1. In a large saucepan, cover the potatoes and garlic with water. Bring to a boil, reduce the heat, cover, and cook 15 to 20 minutes, or until tender. Reserve ¼ cup cooking water. Drain the potatoes.

2. Return the hot potatoes and garlic to the pan. Mash until smooth with a potato masher. Stir in the spinach and butter until blended, adding the cooking water as needed if too stiff. Heat the mixture over low heat, stirring, until hot. Stir in the cheese, salt, and pepper.

Mashed Browns

These are faster to make than hash browns, as you don't need to peel or dice the potatoes. A combination of Yukon Gold, red-skinned, and blue potatoes are pretty, but you can use whatever kind you have on hand. Serve these with bacon and scrambled eggs for a soul-satisfying breakfast or brunch.

1½ pounds all-purpose potatoes, cut into 1-inch chunks
2 tablespoons butter
1 tablespoon olive oil
1 small onion, chopped
½ cup finely diced red bell pepper
½ cup finely diced green bell pepper
½ teaspoon salt
¼ teaspoon freshly ground pepper
⅛ teaspoon cayenne

1. Place the potatoes in a large saucepan and add enough cold water to cover by 1 inch. Bring to a boil, reduce the heat, cover, and cook 10 minutes, or until just tender. Drain the potatoes.

2. In a large nonstick skillet, heat the butter and oil over medium heat. Return the potatoes to the saucepan. With a potato masher, coarsely mash the potatoes, leaving them chunky. Add the potatoes, onion, red and green bell peppers, salt, pepper, and cayenne to the skillet.

3. Cook the mixture, turning occasionally and pressing with a spatula, until the potatoes are browned and crusty, 15 to 20 minutes.

Mashed Sweet
Potatoes

Sweet potatoes are the stars here. Darker skinned, orange-fleshed sweet potatoes are used for these recipes. Sweet potatoes are a great source of beta-carotene and vitamin C, and they certainly don't have to be drowned in butter and sugar to be delicious. Sweet potatoes are naturally sweet and are wonderful all on their own.

Here Curried Sweet Potatoes are flavored with onions, ginger, garlic, peas, and yogurt. Bourbon-Spiked Sweet Potato and Pear Puree is silky smooth, sweetened subtly with roast pear and just a touch of brown sugar, a grown-up sweet potato dish if ever there was one. Golden Buttermilk Mashed Potatoes are a low-fat combination of sweet and baking potatoes mashed with buttermilk. Think of Mashed Sweet Potatoes with Vinegar-Glazed Shallots for a serious dinner. And Roast Sweet Potato Mash with Apples and Maple Syrup, moistened with cider, is made for fall, especially at Thanksgiving.

Curried Sweet Potatoes with Browned Onions, Ginger, and Peas

These spicy sweet potatoes go well with simple roast chicken or turkey. If you love curry, consider them for a light vegetarian lunch.

2 pounds sweet potatoes, peeled and quartered

2 tablespoons butter

1 medium onion, finely chopped

2 teaspoons finely grated fresh ginger

1 garlic clove, crushed through a press

2 teaspoons curry powder

½ cup frozen tiny peas

½ cup plain low-fat yogurt

¾ teaspoon salt

1. In a large saucepan, cover the potatoes with water. Bring to a boil, reduce the heat, cover, and cook 15 to 20 minutes, or until tender.

2. In a medium skillet, melt the butter over medium heat. Add the onion and cook, stirring often, until soft and browned, 8 to 10 minutes. Add the ginger, garlic, and curry powder and cook 1 minute, stirring constantly. Stir in the peas. Set the skillet aside.

3. Drain the potatoes well in a colander. Return the hot potatoes to the saucepan and mash with a potato masher until smooth. Add the yogurt and mash until fluffy. Stir in the onion mixture and salt.

Bourbon-Spiked Sweet Potato and Pear Puree

Serves 6

The roasted pear gives this velvety puree a sweet touch, and bourbon adds a nice jolt. *(Dark rum or orange juice can be substituted for the bourbon.) Here's a recipe that can be "mashed" in the food processor.*

4 medium sweet potatoes (2 pounds)
1 large firm-ripe Bartlett pear, halved lengthwise
½ cup pecans
3 tablespoons butter
2 tablespoons bourbon
2 tablespoons dark brown sugar
½ teaspoon salt
⅛ teaspoon pepper

1. Preheat the oven to 400°F. Prick the potatoes and bake 1 hour, or until soft. Place the pear halves cut sides down in a buttered pie plate and place in the oven after 35 minutes, baking the pear 25 minutes, or until tender.

2. Reduce the oven temperature to 350°F. Place the pecans on a baking sheet and bake 8 minutes, or until fragrant and toasted. Let cool, then coarsely chop.

3. Halve the potatoes and scoop into a food processor. Remove the core from the pear halves, cut the pear into chunks, and add to the processor. Puree the potatoes and pears until smooth. Add the butter, bourbon, brown sugar, salt, and pepper. Puree until blended.

4. Turn the puree into a saucepan and stir over low heat until hot. Turn it into a serving dish and garnish with the toasted pecans.

Mashed Sweet Potatoes with Vinegar-Glazed Shallots

Serves 4

Roasting instead of boiling the sweet potatoes intensifies their flavor. This is a simple way to dress up mashed sweet potatoes.

3 large sweet potatoes
2 tablespoons butter
3 large shallots, sliced
1 tablespoon sugar
2 teaspoons balsamic vinegar
½ teaspoon salt
⅛ teaspoon freshly ground pepper

1. Preheat the oven to 400°F. Prick the potatoes with a fork. Place on a baking sheet and roast 1 hour, or until soft.

2. While the potatoes bake, melt 1 tablespoon of the butter in a medium skillet over medium-low heat. Add the shallots. Cook, stirring frequently, until lightly browned, about 4 minutes. Cover and cook 6 minutes longer, or until soft. Stir in the sugar and vinegar and cook, stirring constantly, until the vinegar evaporates and the shallots are glazed, 1 to 2 minutes. Remove from the heat.

3. Remove the potatoes from the oven and let stand 5 minutes. Cut in half lengthwise. Holding the potatoes with a kitchen mitt or pot holder, scoop the pulp into a food processor. Add the remaining tablespoon of butter, salt, and pepper. Puree until smooth. Turn the potatoes into a bowl and stir in half of the shallots. Garnish with the remaining shallots.

Roast Sweet Potato Mash with Apples and Maple Syrup

Serves 6

Apples, *apple cider, and maple syrup say autumn for sure. After roasting, everything is mashed together right in the roasting pan. This dish goes particularly well with roast pork. You can use 2 tablespoons chopped onion instead of the shallot.*

3 tablespoons butter

3 large sweet potatoes (2¼ pounds), peeled and cut into 1-inch chunks

2 large McIntosh apples, peeled, cored, and thickly sliced

1 shallot, minced

3 tablespoons pure maple syrup

¾ teaspoon salt

⅛ teaspoon freshly ground pepper

⅓ cup apple cider

1. Preheat the oven to 400°F. Place the butter in a shallow roasting pan. Place the pan in the oven until the butter is melted. Add the potatoes, apples, shallot, maple syrup, salt, and pepper. Toss until combined. Spread everything out and cover the pan with foil. Bake 30 minutes. Uncover and bake 10 to 15 minutes longer, or until the vegetables and apple slices are soft.

2. Add the apple cider to the roasting pan and mash the mixture with a potato masher until smooth. Return the pan to the oven to heat the potatoes through, about 5 minutes.

Golden Buttermilk Mashed Potatoes

These creamy potatoes will make all potato lovers happy, as they combine both white and sweet potatoes. They are also great for calorie watchers because they are low in fat.

1½ pounds baking potatoes, peeled and quartered

¾ pound sweet potatoes, peeled and quartered

2 garlic cloves, sliced

¾ cup buttermilk

¾ teaspoon salt

⅛ teaspoon freshly ground pepper

1 tablespoon minced chives or scallions

1. Place the baking potatoes, sweet potatoes, and garlic in a large saucepan and add enough water to cover by 1 inch. Bring to a boil, reduce the heat, cover, and cook 15 to 20 minutes, or until tender. Reserve ¼ cup cooking water and drain the potatoes and garlic well in a colander.

2. Transfer to a large bowl and mash with a potato masher or large spoon. With an electric mixer on medium speed, gradually beat in the buttermilk until the potatoes are smooth and fluffy, beating in the reserved cooking water if necessary. Beat in the salt and pepper.

3. Reheat the potatoes if necessary, turn into a serving dish, and sprinkle the chives on top.

Index